How To Beat The Dealer At Any Casino

AMERICAN PUBLISHING

Printed in the United States of America

0 9 8 7 6 5 4 3 2 1

ISBN NUMBER1-884350-84-4

Table of Contents

Chapter 3   Simplified Card Counting System   47

HOW TO BEAT THE DEALER AT ANY CASINO

Introduction

Why a book on Blackjack? Why not Craps, Roulette or some other popular casino game? After all, the odds of winning any casino game are slim to none at all, right?

Taken at face value, those questions are understandable. After all, gamblers wager hundreds of billions of dollars every year in casinos across the United States, and very few of them actually ever "beat the house". That's because most casinos around the world need to rake in more than a million dollars a day in winnings just to break even. And any casino, anywhere in the world wants to do more than just break even - a whole lot more. That's why casinos stack the deck in their own favor with games like Craps and Roulette where the house always has the advantage.

There is one game, however where all casinos are vulnerable. And that game is Blackjack— the most popular casino table game from Atlantic City to the Strip in Las Vegas. Nearly $90 billion a year is wagered at Blackjack tables in The United States alone. Unfortunately for most gamblers, those wagers are little more than "sucker's bets", because they rely on hunches or 'lady luck" to beat the dealer. And the casinos are more than happy to keep these players in the dark about their secret vulnerability to a skilled Blackjack player.

Blackjack is the only casino game where a skilled player can actually turn the odds in his favor and consistently beat the house for big winnings. And there's no hocus pocus, no card tricks, no lady luck, no intuition involved. The secret to beating the dealer at Blackjack is in learning the techniques of proper play — learning a simple system that shows the player how to bet his money properly and how to play each hand properly. This is accomplished through mastering basic strategies for playing and a simple technique called card counting.

How To Beat The Dealer At Any Casino

The system described on the following pages of this book combines both elements of winning blackjack - proper playing strategies and a simple card counting system. The basic strategy for play allows the player to overcome the house advantage and play the dealer on an even keel. The simple card counting system takes it to the next level and gives the player an advantage over the casino. And that's what this book is all about — a simple system, that if properly employed, will allow any player to gain the advantage at the Blackjack table and actually beat the casino - any casino!

The system you will learn on the following pages doesn't require the brainpower of Albert Einstein or the 2+ gigabyte memory of a Pentium computer. You don't need a math degree to use this system and beat the casino. Anyone who understands and applies the principles of basic strategy and who can count up and down by ones will be able to use the simple (yet scientific) system described in this book The basic strategies for proper play and the simplified card counting system you'll learn are based on mathematical probabilities. There's no guesswork involved. The system has been analyzed and tested through billion and billions of Blackjack hands. And because this system works - and works well - casino operators are terrified. They will do anything in their power to figure out who you are and stop you. If you sit down at a Blackjack table unprepared, you could quickly find yourself banned from the casino.

How To Beat The Dealer At Any Casino

Casinos are constantly on the lookout for counters, so learning and mastering our system of beating the dealer is just the beginning. So, here's what you'll learn on the following pages:

1) Basic Strategy For Proper Play - Basic strategy is the proper or correct way to play each hand of Blackjack based only on the cards you hold and the dealer's upcard. Used properly, basic strategy can help you reduce the house advantage to almost even odds.

2) Simplified Card Counting System - Our simplified system, based on mathematical probabilities, while easy-to-learn and use, is a powerful tool that will enable you to gain information about cards already played so you can determine the favorability of the remaining pack. You need this information in order to make the proper betting strategies work in your favor. Combined with proper play, this counting system will give you the advantage against any casino.

3) Money Management —This chapter provides valuable information about handling your money wisely to insure long-term winnings. You'll learn the best betting strategies, how to bet within your means, how to maximize your gains and minimize your losses, and much more.

4) Casino Secrets — In this chapter you'll learn the proper casino playing tactics to help you disguise your skills and camouflage your abilities as a counter. Your ultimate goal (besides winning) is to be able to play in any casino without being detected as a counter by casino personnel. You'll learn how to act like a gambler (not a counter), what clothes to wear, how to interact with casino personnel, how to control your emotions, what to do in a variety of casino situations and scenarios, and how to handle the situation if you do get caught counting cards.

Blackjack is the only casino game anyone can learn to play and at which he/she can consistently beat the casino. Being a winner requires mastering the basic strategies of proper play and counting cards. The system you will find on the following pages is a complete system with detailed information about how to use basic strategy and our simplified card counting system.

It's an easy, yet powerful system that if used properly can start you on a worldwide journey of winning Blackjack. Our system has been tested in casinos from Vegas to Aruba, and it has been a winner worldwide. Armed with the knowledge provided in this book, you too can beat any casino.

Chapter 1

The History And Rules of Blackjack

Someone once said that knowledge is power. That saying certainly holds true for anyone who wants to win at blackjack. The key to winning consistently at blackjack is in learning and understanding the rules of the game and how they affect your prospects for gaining an advantage over the casino. Simply put, it is essential that you not only know the rules of the game, but how you can use those rules to your advantage. Both experienced players and beginners should study this chapter carefully and become familiar with the most common rules of blackjack.

A Little History

How To Beat The Dealer At Any Casino

You might wonder why you need a history lesson just to play blackjack. Actually, you don't. But the more you know about blackjack, the better your chances of mastering the game and becoming a consistently winning player. Don't worry, there are no dates and boring facts to commit to memory - just a few items of interest that may help you gain a perspective on how the game is played today.

Blackjack isn't new. It's a card-gambling game with a history that goes back several centuries in Europe, where it was called 'Twenty-One". Although details are somewhat murky, the game apparently originated in France, where it is still known today at Vingt-Et-Un (21). Eventually the game came to America and took Horace Greeley's advice and headed west.

In the early days, Poker and Craps were the most popular games in the gambling clubs of the Old West. Twenty-One wasn't nearly as popular with gamblers until a rule change led to a new interest. The gambling clubs offered a 10 to 1 payout to any player who was dealt the ace of spades and a jack in a black suit, and re-named the game Blackjack. The new rule and name change enticed many gamblers away from poker and into a chance for the 10 to 1 payout. The new game of Blackjack survived, but the 10 to 1 payout didn't.

Here in the United States, Blackjack has continued to gain in popularity. The games popularity really began to soar in the 1960s following the discovery by mathematicians and computer experts that the casino advantage could be reduced and potentially eliminated through proper play. Learning the basic strategies (outlined in Chapter 2) of when to hit or stand will come close to evening the odds that typically favor the house. Mastering a card-counting strategy (explained in Chapter 3) will actually get the odds in your favor. And that's what winning is all about!

How The Game Is Played

Casino blackjack is played between a dealer and a group of up to seven players. The game is played at a table, generally set up with seven betting spots, although some have as few as five. A dealer acts for the house or casino and stands behind the table to shuffle and deal the cards. The game usually is played with 1, 2, 6 or 8 standard 52-card decks. The total number of cards, whether one deck or eight decks is known as the pack.

The total value of the hand is the sum of the individual cards making up the hand. Those values are:

1) Face cards (e.g. 10, Jack, Queen, King) count as 10.
2) Aces count as either one or 11 (player's choice)

3) All other cards count as their face value.

A game begins with each player placing a bet. In games using multiple decks, the dealer pulls cards from a plastic or wooden box called a shoe. Otherwise, he deals from his hand. The first two player cards are dealt, beginning to the dealer's left and continuing clockwise, face down for single-deck games and face up for multi-deck games. The dealer receives one card face down and the rest face up.

After receiving the first card, each player can hit, or draw cards until they want to stop drawing cards, or stand, or until the hands goes over 21, or busts. Players have the option of hitting or standing on any card total of 21 or below.

Once all players have completed their turns, the dealer must draw cards as long as his card total is less than 16. The dealer must stand when his card total is 17 or more, unless casino rules allow the dealer to hit on a soft 17 (an ace and a 6).

Winning And Losing

Even though there may be as many as six other players in the game, your goal (as is the goal of all other players) is to beat the dealer. To do that, you must hold a hand that is equal to or less than 21 that also beats the dealer's hand. If your first two cards total 21 (blackjack) and the dealer does not have blackjack, you win immediately. If your card total exceeds 21 (bust) or the dealer has a hand of 21 or under that is greater than your hand, then you lose your bet. If you stand with any card total under 21 and the dealer's hand exceeds 21, then you win your bet.

In the event of a tie — you and the dealer have the same card total-the result is called a push, and neither side wins.

Beating the dealer with any hand less than blackjack (21) pays even money. However, if you have blackjack and the dealer does not, it pays 3 to 2.

Placing Your Bet

Once you've decided upon the game you want to play - single deck, multi-deck, etc. — , and before play begins, you (and all other players) must place your bet in the betting space (typically a circle) on the table, in front of your seat. The minimum bet you can make ranges from of low of $1 to as much as $500. The most common minimum bets are $2, $5, and $25. The maximum bet typically varies from $25 to $2,000 +. The most common maximum bet is $500.

Except for using some basic strategy, such as splitting pairs, doubling down and insurance (which I'll explain later), your initial bet will remain unchanged until the conclusion of the hand.

The Deal

Once all bets have been placed, the blackjack dealer shuffles the cards (if he's dealing more than two decks, the shuffled cards will be placed in a box known as a shoe). The dealer then asks a player to cut the deck. Once the deck has been cut, the dealer then discards or "burns" the top card on the deck.

The deal begins with the player seated farthest to the dealer's left (first-base) and proceeds clockwise until the dealer has dealt two cards to each player and to himself. One of the dealer's cards is dealt face down and the other face up. The players receive their first two cards either both face up, or both face down, depending on the casino.

In some casinos, players are allowed to handle the cards. In those games, you'll receive your cards face down, and pick them up with your hands. In other casinos, players' cards are dealt face up, and players are not allowed to touch them. In this type of game, the dealer handles all the cards and chips.

After all initial cards have been dealt the dealer will return to first-base and begin acting on each hand individually. Play continues counterclockwise.

Hitting

Once you have seen your first two cards, you may want to draw another card in an attempt to raise your card total equal to, or as to close to 21 as possible. To signal a hit,
you will tap the table near your cards. The dealer then will deal you another card, face up. Your new total now is the sum of the three cards you have been dealt. You can continue to hit as long as your card total does not go over 21. If you continue to hit and your card total exceeds 21, you bust and immediately lose your wager. For example, let's say your first two cards are 4 and 3 for a total of 7. You hit and receive a 6 as your third card. Your total is now 13 (7+6). You hit again and receive a 9 as your fourth card. Your total now is 22 (13 +9). You hand is busted. You lose.

Standing

If you're satisfied with the hand you've been dealt (it hasn't exceeded 21), you may choose to stand. You do that by moving your hand, palm down over your wager.

Doubling Down

As I noted earlier in this chapter, doubling down is a strategy you can use to change your bet after play has begun. When you double down on your first two cards, you place a matching bet next your original bet and receive one (and only one) additional card, which completes your hand. This strategy, which will be explained in greater detail in Chapter 2, allows you to double your bet under favorable conditions. If you play your cards right, that is.

Splitting Pairs

Splitting is another way to increase your bet under favorable conditions once play has begun. You can split when your first two cards are a pair of any kind (two 7s, two 9s, etc.), or have the same value (10, Q). To do so, you separate the identical or same value cards, leaving them face up, and place an amount of chips equal to your original bet in front of your new hand. You then proceed to play each hand independently, hitting or standing as desired. You can win, lose, or bust with either or both hands.

Surrender

Many casinos offer the option of surrender. Generally, American casinos offer what is called late surrender, wherein if the dealer does not have blackjack, each player has the option of ending his hand by surrendering. When a player surrenders, he loses only half of his original bet. Surrendering is only an option after a player has received his first two cards and before he has signaled for a hit.

When a player surrenders, the dealer takes his cards and half of his original bet. While it isn't usually to a player's best advantage to surrender, it can be useful when the player's hand is weak (e.g., a 16) and the dealer is showing a strong upcard, such as an ace.

Insurance

When the dealer's upcard is an ace, he will ask the players if they want to buy insurance. This is actually a secondary bet - you are, in effect betting that the dealer does indeed have a blackjack.

If you opt to take out insurance, you'll be required to place up to half of your original bet in the area marked on the table. The dealer will then check his hole card to see if he does have a blackjack. If he does, you will be paid off at 2 to 1, however, you'll also lose your original bet. If the dealer does not have blackjack, you lose the insurance bet and play continues as normal.

Taking insurance is not a good strategy to employ unless you are counting cards and know exactly when it is to your advantage to do so.

Summary

■ **Object of the game** — The player attempts to beat the casino, represented by the dealer, by getting a hand total that is equal to or less than 21, and that is higher than the dealer's.

■ **Card values** — Each card has the same value as its face except for the ace and the picture cards. All 10s and picture cards are valued at 10. The ace can be used as either 1 or 11, at the option of the player. Suits have no value whatsoever in blackjack.

■ **Number of players** — Typically from one to eight decks are used in blackjack. The game has a dealer (representing the casino) and from one to seven players.

■ **Number of decks** — The number of decks used varies widely, from one to eight 52-card packs. Single and double decks are dealt by hand. When three or more decks are used, a device known as a shoe is used to hold the undealt cards.

■ **Blackjacks -** When a player receives an ace and a 10-valued card as his first two cards, he has a blackjack or natural and generally is paid off at 3 to 2. If the player and the dealer both have 21 or blackjack, the player pushes with the dealer and doesn't win or lose any money. The hand is a draw.

■ **The deal -** Each player is dealt two cards in sequence, one at a time. The cards are dealt either face up or face down, depending on the casino rules, in a clockwise direction. The dealer also receives two cards, one face up and one face down.

■ **Player's action —** If, after viewing the first two cards the dealer does not have blackjack, the players are allowed to take certain actions based on their individual hands. If the player desires another card, he can signal the dealer for a hit. The player may take as many hits as he wants as long as his card total doesn't exceed 21 (bust). If the player doesn't want any more cards, he should signal the dealer that he wants to stand.

A player may double the amount of his original bet after looking at his first two cards. When doubling down a player places an additional bet equal to his initial bet and then   receives only one additional card.

If the player's first two cards are identical in value, he may split them by betting an amount equal to his original wager on the second card. The player then draws additional cards on each of the split pairs, playing each hand in turn.

Some casinos in the United States allow players to surrender their first two cards. When a player surrenders his hand, he immediately concedes half of his bet without playing his out.

■ **Busting** — If a player's hand exceeds a total of 21, his hand has busted and he loses his bet regardless of the dealer's total. When a player busts, his cards and his bet are immediately collected by the dealer.

■ **Push -** If the player and the dealer have the same total, and the total is 21 or under, the hand is a tie or draw or push and no money is won or lost.

■ **Insurance -** When the dealer's upcard is an ace the players have the option of making an insurance bet equal to half of the amount of their initial bet. If the dealer has a blackjack, the players will be paid at 2-to-1 on their insurance bet. If the dealer doesn't have blackjack, the insurance bet is lost.

That's it. That's how the game of blackjack is played. But there is much more to learn and understand if you want to be a winning blackjack player. You must know when to take the appropriate action, such as splitting, doubling down, and when to take a hit and when to stand. The foundation for these player actions is proper play or basic blackjack strategy. The following chapter explains basic strategy and how it can help you even the odds with the casino.

Chapter 2

Basic Strategy For Winning Blackjack Play

The foundation of being a winning player at blackjack is to utilize proper basic strategy in playing every hand. There's no equivocation here. Success at blackjack is not the result of intuition. You can not play hunches. You can not rely on lady luck. Like it or not, it's all it the math.

Many years ago, IBM expert Julian Braun, ran nine billion black-jack card combinations based on one-to-eight deck blackjack games. That's right, nine billion! Braun's work helped established the fundamental system now known as the basic strategy for proper play of blackjack. After observing player after player from my perch high above the blackjack table, I consulted a friend who works at a marketing company that runs banks of high-powered IBM computers for data analysis purposes. Combining what I learned from months of observation, with my friend's knowledge of the theory of mathematical probabilities allowed us to analyze another several billion blackjack hands.

Needless to say the results of our analysis confirmed Braun's earlier work and refined our own strategy for winning at blackjack. Let me make this clear, the basic strategy for proper play described in this chapter is largely based on the work of many others. The strategy itself is a product of mathematics and is not subject to a lot of change. What I have discovered from my work in a casino and my subsequent years as a winning player is that there is no room for intuition, gut feelings or guesswork when it comes to using basic strategy. The strategy is based on mathematics and a winning player must make the proper or percentage play each time.

It doesn't matter if you've doubled down an 11 against a dealer's 10 six times in a row and lost. You must make the same play when that hand comes up a seventh time. Consistency and strict adherence to basic strategy is essential to playing a winning game. If you can't resolve to always make the proper play based on basic strategy, you might as well quit reading. However if you are serious about being a big winner at the blackjack table, and you are willing to stick to proper play, even during a losing streak, the information in this chapter is guaranteed to help you "even the odds" against the casino.

The proper play or basic strategy for a blackjack games depends on the rules of the casino where you are playing. The basic strategy you would use for a single-deck game in Reno, is somewhat different than the strategy used in a multiple-deck game in Atlantic city. The fundamental strategy described in this chapter is based on conditions where multiple-decks are in play.

I can't stress this enough: the basic strategy must be followed exactly. There's absolutely no margin for hunches, superstition, guessing or blind luck. Sure, you'll lose from time to time. You may even lose several hands in a row. But if you stick strictly to proper play in every situation, in the long run, you'll come out a winner. You must have faith in the mathematics. Don't allow your emotions to guide your play. That's what the casino counts on. Don't prove them right.

One more thought before I proceed. The information and basic strategy tables in this chapter may seem daunting. Sure there's a lot to take in before you can be a winner at blackjack. But the task isn't as impossible as it may initially seem. It really doesn't take days, months or years to memorize the information provided in this chapter. All it requires is that you understand the basic rules and mathematics involved in the game of casino blackjack. Once you understand the reasons behind basic strategy, you'll be able to apply that strategy in any situation, without giving it much thought. That's right, proper play will become automatic. You won't need to consult charts or flash cards to know what action you should take. If you're willing to focus solely on the steps involved in proper play, and are willing to apply those steps consistently, regardless of the immediate outcome, your long-term results are guaranteed to be profitable.

Casino Advantage Versus Player Advantage

It may surprise you to know that in spite of all the money a casino rakes in from blackjack, the house has only one advantage over the player. That single advantage is based on the fact that the player must act first. Granted, that's no small advantage. A player can lose the game before the dealer has even completed his own hand. By acting first, a player may bust before the dealer has received his second card. If the player and dealer both bust, the dealer wins. And keep in mind that the average player busts at least 15% of the time. Advantage casino.

What too few players realize is that the player has several

counter measures or, if you will, potential advantages over the casino. Here are the player advantages in casino blackjack:

■ A player may stand with any total. The dealer must hit or stand according to casino rules.

■ A player may split cards. The dealer cannot.

■ A player may double down on any two cards except blackjack. The dealer cannot deal down.

■   A player may take insurance. This is especially advantageous to a card counter. The dealer may not take insurance.

■ A player receives payment of 3 to 2 if he gets blackjack.

■   A player may vary his bet.

The basic strategy described in this chapter is designed to take maximum advantage of these player options. Players who apply the information found in the following tables can utilize these options and reduce the house advantage down to nearlyodds. And that's an advantage no serious player can afford to ignore.

Hitting Or Standing

How To Beat The Dealer At Any Casino

One thing I witnessed over and over during my time spent in that little room above the blackjack table (besides the babes in low cut gowns) was the number of players who would hit or stand solely on the basis of the card totals they were holding. Apparently, the dealer's upcard had little if any bearing on these players' decisions. Guess what ... these players almost always left the table as losers.

Adhering strictly to basic strategy, that is utilizing the optimal method of play, means that your decision to hit or stand must be based not only on the cards you are holding but on the dealer's upcard, as well. You must always consider the dealer's upcard when deciding whether to hit, stand, double down, split, or surrender. For example, while you may be tempted to automatically hit a hand of 12, consider the dealer's upcard. If the dealer is showing a 4, 5, or 6, your odds of winning are better if you stand. That's because the dealer must hit on 16, and obviously has a good chance of busting. You can use this rule to your advantage by understanding when to stand, even if your card total is far short of 21.

Let me say this again: winning at blackjack requires a strict adherence to basic strategy and that means a through understanding of your hand's potential versus the threat posed by the dealer's upcard. Your playing strategy should depend on these

How To Beat The Dealer At Any Casino

factors alone. No hunches. No guessing. The degree of threat posed by a dealer's upcard generally can be described as follows:

Dealer's Upcard	Potential Threat
Ace	Bad news. A loss is likely.
10 to King lucky to push.9	Still in big trouble. You may be Lesser degree of danger, but you could still be in trouble.
7 to 8	You can afford a smile now. The dealer is beatable.
4 to 6	The dealer is in danger here. The odds are in your favor.
2 to 3 caution.	This is a toss-up. Proceed with

The degree of threat posed by the dealer's upcard isn't determined by intuition or guesswork. It's based on simple arithmetic. For example, the number of 10s and face cards (which account for 16 out of every 52 cards) makes the dealer extremely vulnerable when showing an upcard of 4, 5, or 6. The dealer's hole card is likely to put his hand at 12 to 16, forcing a hit, which is likely to result in a bust. Understanding the degree of threat the

dealer's upcard poses and making your play based on that understanding is essential to winning at blackjack.

Hard Hand Basic Strategy

Figure 1 shows the basic strategy for hitting and standing when playing a hard hand (a hand without an ace, or with an ace that counts as one). Most players find it easier to memorize the strategy tables if they understand why the various plays are

Figure 1   **S = Stand**   **H = Hit**

Player Hand	Dealer's Up Card									
	2	3	4	5	6	7	8	9	10	Ace
17	S	S	S	S	S	S	S	S	S	S
16	S	S	S	S	S	H	H	H	H	H
15	S	S	S	S	S	H	H	H	H	H
14	S	S	S	S	S	H	H	H	H	H
13	S	S	S	S	S	H	H	H	H	H
12	H	H	S	S	H	H	H	H	H	H
4-11	H	H	H	H	H	H	H	H	H	H

made. Once you understand the reasons behind the strategy, knowing when to hit or stand, or make any other play available, memorizing the tables should be a snap.

Looking at the table in Figure 1, and keeping in mind the degree of threat posed by the dealer's upcard, you should note the following:

1) Always hit a hand with a hard total of 11 or less. You can not bust.

2) Always stand with a hard hand with a card total of 17 or higher.

3) If your hand totals 13 to 16, hit against the dealer's up card of 7 or higher, otherwise stand.

4) If your hand totals 12, you should always hit, unless the dealer is very weak, showing a 4 to 6, and therefore more likely to bust.

Soft Hand Basic Strategy

Your decision whether or not to hit also depends on whether or not you're holding an ace. A hand with an ace, which can be changed in value from 11 to one if necessary, is called a soft hand. Taking hits when holding a soft hand generally is less risky that taking hits with a hard hand. Figure 2 shows the basic

FIGURE 2

Player Hand	Dealer's Up Card									
	2	3	4	5	6	7	8	9	10	Ace
A,8-10	S	S	S	S	S	S	S	S	S	S
A,7	S	S	S	S	S	S	S	H	H	H
A,2-6	H	H	H	H	H	H	H	H	H	H

S= Stand　　　　　　　**H= Hit**

strategy based on a soft hand and the dealer's upcard.

The basic strategy for hitting and standing with a soft hand, as shown in Figure two can be summed up as follows:

1) Always stand with a soft 19 or better ... that is any hand with 19 to 21.

2) With a soft 18 (ace and a 7), always hit against a dealer's 9 or better, otherwise stand (unless doubling).

3) Always hit with a soft 17 or less (ace and a 6 or less)

Generally, you won't hit a 17 or 18. However, the flexibility of the ace in soft hands allows you to hit when you obviously wouldn't

Figure 3   Double Down A Hard Hand

Player Hand	Dealer's Up Card									
	2	3	4	5	6	7	8	9	10	Ace
12	D	D	D	D	D	D	D	D	D	D
11	DD	DD	DD	DD	DD	DD	DD	DD	DD	D
10	DD	DD	DD	DD	DD	DD	DD	DD	D	D
9	DD	DD	DD	DD	DD	D	D	D	D	D
8	D	D	D	D	D	D	D	D	D	D

DD = Double Down   D = Don't Double Down

with a hard hand of the same value.

Doubling Down   Hard Hand Basic Strategy

The option of doubling down is an advantage that a player has over the dealer. It's a powerful play because it allows you to increase your bet after seeing favorable cards. Used judiciously, doubling down can help "even the odds" and offset the house advantage. However, you must know when it's proper play to double down. Statistically, doubling down is a smart move when your hand totals 9 to 11, because a ten value card could give you 19 or 21.

The table in Figure 3 shows when you should double down with a hard hand.

1) With a hard nine, double down against a dealers 3 through 6.

2) Double down with a hard ten if the dealer shows a 9 or less. While it's true that a dealer 9 is strong, the statistical advantage is still in your favor.

3) Double and 11, unless the dealer's upcard is an ace.

4) Never double down with a hard eight, or less.

Doubling Down Soft Hand Basic Strategy

Figure 4 shows the recommended basic strategy for doubling down a soft hand. The basic strategy here is to take advantage of a weak dealer up card (4 through 6). In blackjack it's Ok to kick the dealer when he's down. In fact, it's proper play! However, don't get carried away. You never want to double down if you have a hand totaling 19 or 20,

because you run the risk of ruining your already strong hand.

Basic strategy for doubling down with a soft hand, shown in Figure 4, is as follows:

1) Never double down (or hit) on 19 or 20. The hand's too strong.

2) With a soft 17 or 18, double down against the dealer's 3 through 6.

3) With a soft 15 or 16, double down against the dealer's 4

Figure 4   Double Down A Soft Hand

DD = Double Down   D = Don't Double Down

Player Hand	Dealer's Up Card									
	2	3	4	5	6	7	8	9	10	Ace
A ,8,9	DD	DD	DD	DD	DD	DD	DD	DD	DD	DD
A,6-7	DD	D	D	D	D	DD	DD	DD	DD	DD
A, 4-5	DD	DD	D	D	D	DD	DD	DD	D	D
A, 2-3	DD	DD	DD	D	D	DD	D	D	D	D

through 6.

4) With a soft 13 or 14, double down only when the dealer has the highest probability of busting, with a very weak up card of 5 through 6.

Insert at the top.

Splitting Pairs Basic Strategy

The option to split pairs is another important advantage a player has over the dealer. In fact, if you don't split when the cards warrant doing so, the house advantage rises dramatically. That's no way to play winning blackjack. Used properly, splitting pairs is one of the most powerful weapons you have to wield against the dealer. When used in strict accordance with basic strategy, splitting pairs is worth nearly .5% to the player. And

Figure 5   **Spliting Pairs Basic Strategy**

Player Hand	Dealer's Up Card									
	2	3	4	5	6	7	8	9	10	Ace
A,A	S	S	S	S	S	S	S	S	S	S
10,10	DS	DS	DS	DS	DS	DS	DS	DS	DS	DS
9,9	S	S	S	S	S	DS	S	S	DS	DS
8,8	S	S	S	S	S	S	S	S	S	S
7,7	S	S	S	S	S	S	DS	DS	DS	DS
6,6	S	S	S	S	S	DS	DS	DS	DS	DS
5,5	DS	DS	DS	DS	DS	DS	DS	DS	DS	DS
4,4	DS	DS	DS	S	S	DS	DS	DS	DS	DS
3,3	S	S	S	S	S	S	DS	DS	DS	DS
2,2	S	S	S	S	S	S	DS	DS	DS	DS

S = SPLIT   **DS = DON'T SPLIT**

that's an advantage you can't afford to blow.

The biggest advantage of splitting pairs is that it allows you to double your bet in a favorable situation.

The table shows the basic strategy for splitting pairs.

1) **Always split a pair of aces.** Your odds of getting two very high hands (possibly two 21s) are very good.

2) **Never split a pair of 10s.** I've seen this misguided play many times. Splitting tens is a good way to ruin an excellent hand.

3) **Split 9s against a dealer's 9 or less, except 7**. It's best to split 9s when the dealer is showing a relatively weak upcard of 2 through 6, so that you can leverage the dealer's weakness with an additional bet. If the dealer shows an 8, then you split 9s, because you might get hit with 10s, which would give you winners (19s versus the dealer's 18). If the dealer shows a 9 upcard, then you split the cards because the dealer likely has a 19, which beats your 18 if you stand. Splitting 9s against a dealer's upcard of 7, is statistically a bad move, because the dealer may end up standing pat with a 17, which you've already beat with your pair of 9s (18).

4) Always split eights. With a pair of 8s, it's always a wise play to split against the dealer now matter what his upcard, ace included. At first you might think it's foolish to split against an ace and risk losing twice the money. However, by not splitting, you're left holding a very weak 16. And that, friend, is almost a guaranteed loser. Splitting 8s against a dealer's ace is basically a defensive strategy. While it will increase your chances of winning ever so slightly, it also will help you get out of the hand with as littler loss as possible.

5) Only split 7s against a dealer's upcard of 7 or less. While a hand of 14 is weak, starting two new hands with 7 could result in two 17s. If the dealer shows 8 or better, then you should stand because you're better off losing one bet against the dealer's likely 18 to 21 vs. your paltry 14 than losing two bets (dealer's 18 to 21 vs. your likely two 17s).

6) Split a pair of 6s against a dealer's 6 or less.

7) Never split 5s. A pair of 5s combine for a strong 10. Split, they'll likely get hit with a 10, leaving you with two lousy hands and at least one probable bust.

8) Split 4s only when the dealer is showing a weak 5 or 6. Splitting 4s will result in two crummy hands (catching 10s will make them a miserable 14). You should only split 4s when the dealer is in a more vulnerable position that you are (showing a 5 or 6).

9) Split 2s and 3s against a dealer's upcard of 7 or less.

Basic Strategy And Buying Insurance

If you buy insurance, you're betting on the probability of the dealer having blackjack. You can only buy insurance when the dealer's upcard is an ace. If you're scared silly that the dealer does indeed have a blackjack, you can buy insurance and bet half of your original bet that the dealer has blackjack. If he does, the bet pays 2 to 1. However, you lose your original or main bet (unless, of course, you also have a natural and push).

The thing to remember here is that buying insurance neither increases nor decreases your chances of winning your original bet. That means that taking insurance is strictly a side bet. The main hand will be played to its completion regardless what happens with the side bet. The insurance bet doesn't insure anything on the main hand.

Basic strategy says NEVER TAKE INSURANCE. Unless you are an expert at counting cards (see Chapter 3 Card Counting) and know the deck is extremely rich in 10-value cards, the odds are not in your favor and you should not make an insurance bet.

Basic Strategy And Surrendering

Late surrender is the only option we are interested in. In late surrender, the dealer first checks his hole card for blackjack. Late surrender is only advisable when your chances of busting are very high, and the dealer has a particularly strong upcard. Here are the basic strategy plays for surrendering:

1) Surrender on 16: f the dealer's upcard is a 9 to an ace, save half your bet and surrender. The dealer most likely has a strong hand (19 to 21) and you will probably bust if you hit.

2) Surrender on a 15: If you're holding a 15, only surrender when the dealer's upcard is a ten. If the3 dealer's upcard is an ace, it's better to hold on than to surrender. The dealer must reveal blackjack (if he has it) before you surrender. So, if the dealer is showing an ace, and he hasn't revealed a blackjack, you already know that he doesn't have a 10-value hole card. You can beat many of the dealer's possible hole cards, so don't surrender, continue to play.

3) Surrender on 14. No matter how tempted you are, do not surrender on 14. Despite the prevalence of 10-value cards, your odds of drawing a 7 to ace are actually pretty good.

Basic Strategy Master Chart

Figure 7 shows the chart for all the basic strategies presented in this chapter. The chart combines all the strategies and shows whether you should hit, stand, double down, or split pairs based on your hand and the dealer's upcard. While the individual charts for each strategy are extremely useful, the master chart has proven to be a highly functional memorization tool. At first glance the chart may look scary, but trust me, with a little practice and patience you will come to know the information in this chart as well as your own name.

Actually, you won't be memorizing the chart itself, you'll be converting the information it provides into some basic strategy rules. For example, look at the player's hand of a pair of aces in Figure 7 (Blackjack Basic Master Chart). The chart shows that you should always split aces, regardless of the dealer's upcard. You can turn that information into a simple, basic rule: "Always split a pair of aces". You can do that with each player's starting hand until you've mastered the basic strategy rules.

To use the Master Chart in Figure 7, simply locate your two-card hand in the leftmost column then move across the chart to the corresponding dealer upcard. Another example: If you are dealt ace, 6 (soft 17) against the dealer's 7, you should hit.

How To Beat The Dealer At Any Casino

H= Hit   S= Stand   Sp = Split   D = Double

PLAYER HAND	DEALER UP CARD									
	2	3	4	5	6	7	8	9	10	A
5	H	H	H	H	H	H	H	H	H	H
6	H	H	H	H	H	H	H	H	H	H
7	H	H	H	H	H	H	H	H	H	H
8	H	H	H	H	H	H	H	H	H	H
9	D	D	D	D	H	H	H	H	H	H
10	D	D	D	D	D	D	D	D	H	H
11	D	D	D	D	D	D	D	D	D	H
12	H	S	S	S	H	H	H	H	H	H
13	S	S	S	S	H	H	H	H	H	H
14	S	S	S	S	H	H	H	H	H	H
15	S	S	S	S	H	H	H	H	H	H
16	S	S	S	S	H	H	H	H	H	H
17+	ALWAYS STAND									

a dealer's upcard of 7,

otherwise stand

✓ With 12, stand against a dealer's upcard of 4 through six, otherwise hit.

✓ With 11 or less, always hit, unless doubling.

How To Beat The Dealer At Any Casino
BLACKJACK BASIC STRATEGY MASTER CHART

PLAYER HAND	DEALER UP CARD									
	2	3	4	5	6	7	8	9	10	A
A & 2	H	H	H	D	D	H	H	H	H	H
A & 3	H	H	H	H	H	H	H	H	H	H
A & 4	H	H	H	H	H	H	H	H	H	H
A & 5	H	H	H	H	H	H	H	H	H	H
A & 6	H	D	D	D	D	H	H	H	H	H
A & 7	D	D	D	D	D	D	D	D	D	H
A & 8	D	D	D	D	D	D	D	D	D	D
A & 9	H	H	S	S	S	H	H	H	H	H

H = Hit   S = Stand   Sp = Split   D = Double

PAIRS

PLAYER HAND	DEALER UP CARD									
	2	3	4	5	6	7	8	9	10	A
22	SP	SP	SP	SP	SP	SP	H	H	H	H
33	SP	SP	SP	SP	SP	SP	H	H	H	H
44	H	H	H	SP	SP	H	H	H	H	H
55	D	D	D	D	D	D	D	D	H	H
66	SP	SP	SP	SP	SP	H	H	H	H	H
77	SP	SP	SP	SP	SP	H	H	H	H	H
88	SP	SP	SP	SP	SP	SP	SP	SP	SP	SP
99	SP	SP	SP	SP	SP	SP	S	SP	SP	SP
10S	S	S	S	S	S	S	S	S	S	S
AA	SP	SP	SP	SP	SP	SP	SP	SP	SP	SP

Figure   Blackjack Basic Strategy Master Chart

H= Hit   S= Stand   Sp = Split   D = Double

L Always stand with 17 or more.L With 13 through 16, hit against

Never Take Insurance

Using the Master Chart in Figure 7 as a guide, you can convert the plays into the following easy-to-learn and remember set of basic strategy rules:

Soft Hands

* With soft 19 (ace, 8) or more, always stand.
* With soft 18, hit against the dealer's 9 or better, otherwise stand
* With soft 17, always hit

Doubling Down

* With 10 or 11, double down if your card total is greater than the dealer's upcard.

Splitting Pairs

* Always split a pair of aces or 8s.

* Never split a pair of 5s or 10s

Basic Strategy Summary

The basic strategy for playing winning blackjack is based on mathematical probabilities, considering only the cards the player is holding and the dealer's upcard. The strategy consists of a set of basic rules the player should always use. There's no room for intuition or guesswork with this system. While deviation from the basic strategy may result is modest short-term success, serious players can only be successful in the long-run by consistently applying the basic strategy rules for every play. In other words, unless you have more information about deck composition, other than the cards you are holding and the dealer's upcard, NEVER DEVIATE from the basic strategy outlined in the chapter.

By always applying the basic strategies of proper play you can reduce the house advantage down to practically even odds. Additionally, using a simplified card-counting system (explained in Chapter 3) can actually give you the advantage over the casino.

Chapter 3

Simplified Card Counting System

Ok, so now you know how to even the odds against the casino — apply the basic strategy rules to every play based only on the cards you are holding and the dealer's upcard. Now, it's time to take your play to the next level and actually gain the advantage over the casino. The next level involves counting cards.

Several years ago, when I was assigned to "watch over" the blackjack table, my job was to keep the dealers on their toes, and the players honest. Keeping the players "honest" meant I was supposed to be on the lookout for "card-counters". Actually, there's nothing dishonest about counting cards, and card counters are not breaking any law. Any written law, that is. The fact is that every casino in the world has an "unwritten law" when it comes to card counting. Simply put, they frown upon card counting, and generally will eject, even ban any card counters they catch.

From my vantage point above the blackjack table, most card counters were usually easy to spot. The beginners would lose it right way ... disoriented by the actual speed of play, while they tried to keep track of the cards in a multiple-deck game with some complex counting system that would befuddle even experienced players. And therein lies the most common mistake when it comes to counting cards ... you don't need to master some complex scheme or memorize all the cards in a deck. You don't have to be a mathematical genius or have a photographic memory to be successful at counting cards.

If you can count up and down by ones, you can count the cards in a deck, even when playing a multiple deck game. There's no need to make it any more complex than it has to be. In this chapter, I'll describe a simplified card-counting system that can be used when playing single- or multiple-deck games. The system is based on assigning a point value (plus or minus) to each card, adding those point values together as each card is played and then converting that information into a usable form. You then can use the information or cumulative running count to make decisions on betting, playing the hand and in some cases taking insurance (something you are advised never to do when using only the basic strategy described in the last chapter).

This simplified counting system, which has been tested and verified by computer simulations and thousands of hours of actual Blackjack play at casinos throughout the world, is easy to learn and it's easy to use.

A Brief History Of Card Counting

The first accurate counting systems were developed by mathematician Dr. Edward Thorp nearly 40 years ago. Dr. Thorp discovered, through mathematical analysis and computation that the card with the most influence on the deck being in favorable condition for the player was the five. Thorp's computations revealed that when the deck is low in fives, the player has a higher advantage than if it's lacking in any other card. Based on that discovery, a very simple card counting strategy was born. Just keep track of the fives. That was known as the "Five Count" system, which later was revised to include 10s and was subsequently renamed the "Ten Count" system.

How To Beat The Dealer At Any Casino

The Ten Count system was so named because it involved counting 10s versus all other cards in the deck. Using such a counting system, a player began with two numbers, which represented the total number of 10s in a complete pack. For example, in a single-deck game, the player would begin with these two numbers, 36, 16. Those two numbers represent 36 cards in the deck other than 10s, and 16 10s (52 total cards in the deck). Once the game began and the cards were dealt, the player kept track or counted by reducing the appropriate number. If the player received a 9, 10, he would adjust the count to 35, 15. If the dealer's upcard were a 6, the count then would be 34, 15, and so on through the deck.

It was a fairly simple and easy- to- use system. The player would use the running count to calculate (mentally, of course) a ratio of non-10s to 10s, and then use the result to make betting decisions, take insurance and pay the hands. Using the above running count as an example, the ratio of non-10s to 10s would be 34˜15, or 2.27.

You can see that the old Ten Count system was certainly a simple counting method. However, once the casinos started to deal more and more multiple-deck games, the system began to break down. Instead of a single deck, imagine counting down say six decks. Your starting count would be 216, 96 instead of a relatively easy to handle 36, 16. And then try coming up with an accurate ratio for a running count of say 142, 56 in a split second. You get the idea.

Over the years a number of researchers and mathematicians developed a new method of counting based on a simple point count system. Using the new system, counters found it much easier to count down multiple-decks than with the old Ten Count system.

Nowadays there are a number of card counting systems ranging from simple to complex. All are based, to some degree on the point count method. The thing to understand is that the degree of complexity has little bearing on the final results. Typically, a more complex system of counting cards will give you a slightly better advantage, should you master it. That's the problem. Complex systems, while good in theory, aren't really practical when you're sitting at a blackjack table in a noisy, distraction-filled casino. If the system is too complex to use properly under real casino conditions, it's of no use.

The card-counting system described in this chapter is based on and is a variation of the point count method of counting cards. Although a model of simplicity, it's a powerful system that if mastered and applied properly will give you a decided edge against the casino. It's very easy to master. Again if you can count by ones, add and subtract, you'll have no problem mastering this simplified card-counting system.

The Advantage Of Counting Cards

Why count cards? Why not just stick with basic strategies based on the cards you hold and the dealer's upcard? As I've already noted, applying basic strategy mitigates the casino advantage to almost 0%. Counting Cards will help you take the next step and actually get the odds in your favor.

Card counters keep track of the cards as they are dealt, but they pay more attention to the ratios of important cards rather than memorizing exactly which cards are left in the deck. Cards usually are counted in ratios of large cards to small cards. Here's how card counting works: The player gains an advantage when a deck has a shortage of cards valued 2,3,4,5,6,7,8. If a deck has a shortage of cards valued 9, 10, Ace, the player is at a disadvantage. In other words, by knowing what cards remain in the deck or shoe, you can determine when the deck is either favorable to you or to the dealer. Armed with that information, you can bet accordingly. For example, you can bet more money when you know the deck is favorable to you. You also may alter your basic strategy play to account for favorability, thereby increasing the odds of winning a particular game.

And that's it in a nutshell. That's why we count cards - to determine which cards remain to be played. As the game proceeds and the composition of the deck changes, the ratio of good and bad cards swings the advantage back and forth between the player and the casino. The answer is simple, as players, we need to know when the odds are with us and when they aren't. Our betting decisions should be based on that knowledge. We raise our bets when we have the advantage and make smaller bets when we don't. By following such a strategy, the gains from the big bets we make when we have the advantage will completely erase the losses from the smaller bets. And that makes us winners in the long run.

How To Count The Cards

The first thing we need to do is assign point values to each type of card in a deck. With our easy-to-use counting system those values are as follows:

Card	Point Value
2	+1
3	+1
4	+1
5	+1

6	+1
7	0
8	0
9	0
10	-1
J	-1
Q	-1
K	-1
A	-1

The basic strategies described in the preceding chapter assume a balanced deck. As you can see by the point values above, our card counting system also is a balanced system. There are 20 cards in a deck that are valued +1 (2 through 6). There are 16 10-value cards and 4 aces in a deck (20 cards) that are valued at -1. The remaining cards (7, 8 ,9) are neutral, or have a value of zero. So, at the end of the deck, the count should be zero.

For example, after one hand in which a 10, 10, J, Q, A, A is played the count will be -6.

Each of the 6 cards played have a point value of -1, making the total running count for this hand -6. The running count reflects the balance of 10-value cards (and aces) to low cards (2, through 6) as they are dealt.

Another example: The following cards are shown in the course of a hand: 4, 7, A, 10, 9, 10, 2, 10, 5, 10. The first value is +1 (the 4); the second card is 7, which is zero, so disregard it. The next card is -1 (the ace). So after the first three cards the running count is 0 (+1, 0,-1 = 0). The next card is a 10 so the running count is now -1. The next card is a 9 (value 0) so ignore it. The running count is still at -1. Next is a 10, making the running count -2. The next card is a 2 (point value +1), bringing the count down to -1. The next card is a 10, so the count is back at -2. Next is a 5, so the count goes back to -1. The final card played is a 10, which ends the hand with a running count of -2. At the end of a hand, in which ten cards were dealt to the players and the dealer, the running count is -2. That negative number lets you know that you now are at a slight disadvantage. Your next bet should either be the same or one or two units lower.

The above examples assume you are playing a single deck game. To accurately apply the running count, you also must factor in the number of card decks being used. The result of that calculation is called the true count. The true count is derived by dividing the running count by the number of half decks (26 cards per half deck) remaining to be dealt. Generally, the true count is a more accurate indicator than the running count, because it accounts for the total number of decks used in a game. The true count can be calculated at any time, so the running count is the number you need to remember with each hand.

The True Count

To illustrate the importance of the true count, I'll use a single deck of cards in the following example.

Remember the point values assigned (2 through 6 = +1 each); (7, 8, 9 = 0); (10, J, Q, A = -1 each). The deck starts with six-teen (16) 10-point value cards and sixteen low cards (2 through 6). The game features two players and, or course the dealer. At the end of the first hand, we'll assume that the running count is +2. The dealer has a 3, 6 and Q (+1), the first player has a 4, 2, and 10 (+1), and the second player has a 7 and 9 (0). That adds up to a running count of +2, which indicates that there are two more high cards than low cards left in the deck.

A total of eight cards were dealt in the hand, which means that four low cards and two 10-value cards were played. The deck now contains 14 high cards and 12 low cards. The running count of +2 is a favorable player count, but the deck still holds a relatively high number of low cards.

Now assume that after 30 cards have been played the running count remains at +2. That means the deck now holds 10 high cards and eight low cards. While the running count is the same, the deck actually is much more favorable to the player than when only eight cards had been played.

The true count is found with the following equation: True Count = Running count ˜ Number of half decks to be played. After eight cards have been dealt (as in the above example), almost two half decks remain to be played. The running count (+2) divided by 2 equals +1. The running count after eight cards have been played is +2; the true count is +1. You can see that the true count is already more accurate in weighing the higher number of small cards remaining in the deck.

Again, using the above example: After 30 cards have been played, the running count of +2 is divided by 0.5 (half of a deck). The running count after 30 cards is +2; the true count is now +4 (2˜ 0.5 = +4). In this example, where the running count remains at +2, as more cards are played, the true count shifts in favor of the player.

Reading The Count

A positive count (any count with a plus [+] sign) means that more low cards than high cards have been played, so the deck is loaded with high cards, which is more favorable to the player. Such a deck favors the player because he has a better chance of drawing blackjack. That's an important advantage because blackjack pays better to the player (3 to 2) than for the dealer. In addition, when the count is positive, the dealer is more likely to bust, because he must draw on any hand below 17.

A negative or lower count means that more high cards than low cards have been dealt, so the deck is more favorable to the dealer. In other words, the dealer will bust less often with a negative count. A neutral count, that is a count of 0, is neither favorable or unfavorable.

How To Use The Count When Betting

The successful card counter makes use of the count generally in two ways: he adjusts his bet, and he adjusts his basic strategy play. If the true count is positive, the player increases his bet. When the true count is negative, the player will decrease his bet, or simply leave the table, to come back and play another day.

You can use the true count to decide how much to raise or lower your bet. Obviously, you should raise your bet when the count is higher (positive) to take advantage of your increased probability of winning. You can use the following table as a guide for betting based on the true count. Simply multiply the number (your bet) by the amount of the minimum bet.

True Count	Your Bet
Any negative number	1 unit
0	1 unit
+1	2 units
+2	3 units
+3	3 units
+4	4 units
+5	6 units
+6	6 units
+7	8 units
+8	10 units
+9 and above	12 units (or maximum bet)

Here's an example using the above table: After the first hand of a multiple-deck game, the true count is +4 and you just bet a $5 chip. Before the next hand is dealt, you might wager $20 (four units of $5 = $20).

Counting Aces

You can tweak our simple card counting system just a bit by also keeping a separate count of aces. While, as you can probably tell, the running count and true count include aces in the high-card count, it also can be useful to know whether or not the deck is ace-rich, ace-poor, or neutral. Keeping track of the number of aces left in the deck can add to your advantage because you know that a deck that is full of high cards but also ace-poor will yield few blackjacks.

Since a deck holds four aces, the normal distribution is two aces per half deck. So if one ace (or no aces) is dealt in a half deck (on average), the remaining half-deck is ace-rich. When two or more aces are dealt in a half deck (on average), the deck is ace poor. If the true count is positive and the deck is ace-rich, you may want to raise your bet by one unit. However, if the deck is ace-poor, you may want to subtract a unit from your bet.

Card Counting Practice

I'm sure, even my simplified card counting system seems somewhat difficult to master, especially for beginners. Don't worry. As the saying goes, "practice makes perfect". And practice, before you set foot in a casino is essential. You should not try to count cards in a casino until you have this system down pat. Remember what I've already explained: While counting cards is not unlawful, nor is it cheating in any way, casinos don't like card counters. If fact, they will do anything in their power to figure out who you are and stop you, especially if you're winning.

So you should practice this system until you're sure that your counting becomes automatic, and not easy to detect. Here's a practice method I recommend:

Take two or more decks. Then turn, face up one card at a time. Do this slowly at first, gradually picking up speed as you adjust the count one card at a time. When you reach the end of the deck, your count should be zero. If it isn't, start over again. Keep at it until you've got it down cold. Once you've mastered counting cards one-at-a-time, you should move on to counting multiple cards - two, three, and four at a time.

In my experience, it's actually easier to count groups of cards than it is one card at a time, because high cards cancel low cards without having to adjust the count. For example, if the following cards T, T, 2, 8, 3, 9, A, 4,T, 3,6, 5, 8, 7, T are dealt to seven players and the dealer, you would group T,T, 2, 8, 3, 9, which cancel each other (-1, -1, +1, 0, +1, 0= 0). Then group the A, 4, T, 3, which also cancel each other (-1, +1,-1, +1 = 0). And then add +1 for the 6, 5, 7, 8, T (+1 +1, 0, 0 -1 = +1). The running count at the end of this hand is +1.

I also recommend that you practice counting decks (remember the true count equation: true count = running count ˜ number of half decks to be played). Take several decks and set up distinct piles so that you can learn how to judge the number of decks and half decks in a discard pile. Be sure to subtract that number from the total number of cards used, before you apply the equation for determining the true count.

I can't stress enough how important it is that you practice counting cards and decks before you hit a casino. Once you're sitting at a blackjack table with your hard-earned money on the line, there's little if any margin for error. There's also not a lot of time to fumble around mentally trying to count cards and decks and employing basic strategy under real playing conditions. Sometimes you'll come against a super fast dealer, and only the most experienced and proficient counters can keep up without blowing their cover (more on that in a later chapter). Under such circumstances, you may use the time when other players are making their decisions to update your count. However, if the game moves too fast and you're unsure of the count, don't panic. Your best move then is to fall back on the basic strategy for proper play for the remainder of the shoe.

Summary

You use a card counting system to help you determine whether or not a hand is favorable to you. You use that information to make proper betting and playing decisions, which will give you the advantage against the dealer. You bet big when the remaining deck is in your favor-you bet small when the remaining deck favors the dealer. Obviously aces and 10s favor you because naturals pay off at 3 to 2 for the player. Low cards (2, 3, 4, 5, 6) favor the dealer by decreasing his chance of busting. By knowing the ratio of low cards to high cards that remain to be played, you can determine when a hand is favorable to you or the dealer, and base your betting and playing decisions accordingly.

Counting cards in my simplified system is just that... simple. Starting with a count of zero (after the cards have been shuffled), you add one for each low card 2 through 6 that is played. You subtract one for ever 10-value card (including ace) that is played. Your count will not change when you see 7, 8 or 9 because those cards have been assigned a value of zero. These values are reflected in the point value chart below:

2	3	4	5	6	7	8	9	10	J	Q	K	A
+1	+1	+1	+1	+1	0	0	0	-1	-1	-1	-1	-1

Using this simple point count system you can keep a running count of the cards played and those that remain to be played. The running count is accumulated since the last dealer shuffle. Notice that with this balanced counting system, there is the same number of +1 cards as there are -1 cards. That means that at the end of the deck, the running count should be zero.

Simply put, this simplified point count system tells you when the most favorable cards for the player (10s and aces) outnumber the less favorable low cards (2, 3, 4, 5, 6) in the remaining deck or shoe. You need this information in order to make appropriate betting decisions and to maximize your playing strategy.

To accurately determine the favorability or richness of the remaining cards in the deck or shoe, you need to divide your running count (the cards you've seen so far) by the number of half decks that remain to be played to derive a true count. For example, if the running count is + 4 and one deck remains to be played, the true count is + 2. The true count, being a positive number indicates the remaining deck is in your favor, and you should bet accordingly.

Keeping a running count is not nearly as difficult as in may seem initially. Just remember, you are not memorizing each card, you're simply counting by ones, either plus or minus. Practice is the key to mastering this system before you venture into a casino. Take several decks of cards and practice counting them one by one, slowly at first. Once you've got the hang of it (and it won't take long), begin increasing your counting speed and them begin counting the cards in groups, just as they would be dealt in an actual game. The beauty of this counting system is that the high cards cancel the low cards so it's simply a matter of adding or subtracting ones. You see a 6, that's +1. Then you see an ace (-1) that cancels the 6 and you have a count of zero, and so on as each card is dealt.

The most difficult part of this simple card counting system will most likely be counting the decks to be played in order to get the true count. Again, don't worry. With practice counting decks will become second nature, just like counting cards to get the running count. Just don't expect to master this system overnight. I promise it's easy to learn and use, but it does take a good bit of practice before it becomes automatic. And that's what you want. You want to be able to take your place at first base or anywhere else at the blackjack table with complete confidence in your ability not only to utilize the basic strategy for proper play, but to keep an accurate running and true count. In order to win, you need the edge this card counting system gives you.

One final thought, before we head on to a new chapter in your journey to beat the casino. I think I've made it clear that you must practice and learn the system before you risk any of your money in any casino, anywhere. But just in case that point is a little vague, let me be blunt... You can not win consistently at blackjack unless you master the basic strategy and simplified card counting system I've outlined on the previous pages. Understand and learn the system, and then you'll be ready to use your knowledge to gain the advantage and play winning

Chapter 4

Money Management

blackjack at any casino in the world.

This chapter is near and dear to my heart. I've spent a lot of time on the other side of the blackjack table (actually above the table) observing thousands of players practically handing their money to the casino. As a player, I've also seen the same thing, over and over again— people losing their hard-earned dollars needlessly. Now don't get me wrong. I don't always win. There is no system that can guarantee you'll win every hand. What I'm talking about is betting wisely, and just as important, betting within your means.

If you remember little else from this chapter, remember this: Casinos make money because the players allow them to make money. I remember one player in particular. He obviously was inexperienced but full of confidence that he could play hunches and beat the dealer. Of course he didn't. He wound up losing a bundle. And the bundle turned out to be his rent money. Unfortunately, this particular player is not alone. Too many people think they can rely on lady luck and make some fast money at the blackjack table. They enter the casino with a bankroll they can't afford to lose, and then proceed to lose it all.

You can not win at blackjack if you're betting money you can't afford to lose. The best gamblers in the world run into losing streaks. It happens. The difference is, experienced players ... winning players have an established bankroll they can afford to lose. These players never wager money that if lost will affect their lifestyle in any way. They always have a sum set aside that they can afford to lose. They bet only what they can afford to bet and then only when the play warrants it. That's what ultimately separates the winners from the losers. My rule of thumb: If you ain't got it to lose, stay out of the casino.

The Risk Of Playing Blackjack

Ok, sermon's over— now on to the fundamentals of money management. What I mean by money management as it relates to winning at Blackjack is minimizing your losses and maximizing your gains. And to understand what that means, you first have to accept this fact: When you play casino blackjack you risk losing money. The advantage a player has over a casino, when using basic strategy and our simplified counting system is not so great that your bankroll can never take a heavy hit. That's why proper management of your funds is essential in all phases of the game to give you the best possible chance of achieving the most long-term gain.

Some players begin their careers as counters with great success and never shed a tear. Most players, however, begin with a loss and it may take many hours of play before they begin showing a profit. I'm not trying to scare you. That's just the nature of the beast. What I'm trying to impress upon you is that initially, you'll need to learn how to survive at the game until your long term advantage begins to take effect. You'll need to learn how to bet to keep your bankroll from being decimated before your long term edge kicks in. You also need to learn how to keep the profits you make. And that's what this chapter is all about.

Three Sacred Rules Betting Rules For Beginners

You've spent hours practicing counting cards. You've mastered the system to the point that you can keep track of the running count and calculate the true count in a matter of seconds. You're ready to take some of the casino's money, right? Wrong! Practicing strategies and card counting at home is one thing... playing for real in a casino is something else altogether.

Unless you've already spent a good deal of time in a casino, you can't really understand what to expect. Casinos are not libraries. They are full of distractions. Besides the dealer, you'll also be battling bright, flashing lights, the distraction of scantily clad cocktail waitresses, alcohol, other gamblers talking, laughing (or crying) or cheering, pit bosses, the din of non-players who are just there to watch, drink and have a good time, and a myriad of other distractions. Perhaps, during your practice sessions you could turn the radio on, have the TV blaring in the background, encourage the kids to laugh and play as loudly as they can, and you may get some small idea of the noise level you'll encounter in a casino. But until you're actually at a casino, sitting at the blackjack table dropping your chips into the betting circle, you can't really appreciate the overall experience.

Unless you have nerves of steel and laser-like focus, your first attempt to count cards during game conditions in a casino will not be mistake-free. It doesn't matter if you play perfectly at home ... the casino experience is pressure packed and your very real money is on the line. I know this to be true from my own personal experience, not only as a casino spy but sitting at the blackjack table for the first time as a player.

Again, I'm not trying to scare you off. I'm just trying to prepare you for reality. As you get more casino playing experience under your belt, you'll get better and better in real playing conditions. But give yourself some time before you drop your bankroll on the table. It may take you an hour or two for you to become accustomed to the casino surroundings.

For beginners, there's nothing like the first real blackjack card-counting session. Here are my three sacred rules to help you get into the swing of things at the casino before your initial bankroll disappears.

1) Stay with the table minimum until you're comfortable with your surroundings and are confident of the count. Remember, this isn't your kitchen table. This is for real. It's real money you're betting. Count cards, keep track of the running and true count, mentally note the correct plays, but bet the table minimum until you are absolutely certain of your abilities. It may take you a few hours of play to become accustomed to actually sitting at a blackjack table in a crowded, noisy casino. Be conservative until you're certain you have found your comfort zone.

2) Don't Panic. The speed of the dealer may unsettle you at first. If you lose the count during play, stay calm. Bet the table minimum, and fall back onto basic strategy until the next shuffle.

3) Don't throw good money after bad. That means if you're losing don't start betting more money to try to get it all back in one hand. Keep in mind, the object of counting cards is to determine when you have a mathematical advantage over the casino. You should bet more money only when the odds are in your favor. Perhaps it's just human nature that makes us want to bet more money to try and recover a loss. We want to recoup our losses as quickly as possible. Big Mistake. Raising a bet following a loss is not winning strategy ... unless of course the true count is in your favor.

Every card counter has winning and losing sessions at the blackjack table. Don't think of the short-term results. Think long-term. Over the long-term, your advantage will take effect and your winnings will begin to add up. Short-term fluctuations in your bankroll should not determine your long-term money management goals.

Making The Maximum Bet

You should understand by now that as counter you have an advantage over the casino when betting and playing properly. You also should understand that your advantage doesn't guarantee a winning hand each time you play. Your fortunes will fluctuate. You may win a few hands and then you'll run into a losing streak. It happens to the best players. It's in those times that many players overbet in an attempt to compensate for short-term sustained losses. The key to successful money management in blackjack, is to be patient and don't overreact to short-term losses. Remember, your success at blackjack will be determined over the long run. So you must always bet within your means

A good rule of thumb to follow, especially for beginners is to limit your maximum bet to no more than 1% of your total blackjack bankroll. For example, let's say your bankroll is $5,000, then your maximum bet might be $50. By keeping your maximum bet at or below 1% of your total bankroll, you'll reduce the risk of decimating your funds to an acceptable level. Even though you may be certain you have the advantage, don't give in to temptation and overbet. Set a limit on your maximum bet, whether it's 1% of your bankroll or less, and stick to it. You're bound to come out a winner in the long run.

How To Make Winning Betting Decisions

As a counter, all of your betting decisions will (or should) be made based on the true count (as described in the previous chapter). This applies to both multi- and single-deck games. So the more proficient you become at keeping a running count and converting to a true count, the better able you'll be to make proper, and winning betting decisions.

Before I explain how to bet with the true count, here's a brief refresher on determining the true count in a game of blackjack. For this example, I'll use a multi-deck game. If six small cards (2, 3, 4, 5, or 6) are dealt in the first round of the game, you'll have a running count of +6. If you're in a four-deck game, there are just slightly less than four decks remaining to be played. That means the count per remaining deck, or the true count is about 1.5 (running count, 6 ˜ by number of decks remaining to be played, nearly 4).

To estimate the number of remaining decks in a multi-deck

game, your best friend is the discard tray. The discard tray can be found on virtually every blackjack table where there is a multi-deck game being played. As cards are used the dealer places them in the discard tray where every player can see them. Keep your eye on the discard tray at the end of each hand and then do just a bit of subtraction to determine how many decks remain to be played. In a four-deck game, if there are two decks in the discard tray, and no other cards are on the table, there obviously have to be two decks left in the shoe. The goal here is to be accurate to within a half-deck to make the best estimate.

The quick mental subtraction required to arrive at the true count may seem a bit daunting at first. At least it was to me, but I soon discovered that with practice this step becomes automatic. And as you gain more experience, you'll also discover as I did that you'll come to look at the discard tray and simply know how many decks it holds without actually having to do the subtraction. Let's say you're in a six-deck game and you see about 3.5 decks in the tray. You know, automatically, without having to subtract 3.5 from 6, that you have to divide your running count by 2.5 to arrive at the true count. Those are the kinds of mental calculations that will become second nature the more you practice and gain experience.

Betting With The True Count

Now, on to the good stuff... how to beat the casino with proper betting strategy. Consider the true count. For every increase of 1 in the true count, as figured by our plus and minus point value counting system, your advantage over the dealer increases by about .5%. That's in the average blackjack game. Since the casino has an edge over the basic strategy player of .40% it takes a true count of almost 1 in order to get even with the casino. Playing even with the dealer means that a player who employs proper basic strategy will, in the long run, win as much as he loses at a true count of +1. With a true count of +2, the player has an edge of .5% over the casino; a true count of +3 gives the counter an edge of 1%, and so on.

It is the edge or advantage that you have on the upcoming hand that determines your bet. Winning counters bet only a small portion of their bankroll on any one hand, because as I've already noted, while they know they will win in the long run, they also know they can lose any given hand. Small short-term losses are acceptable when taken as part of the big, long-term picture. So, by betting an amount that is in proportion to your advantage (known as the Kelly Criterion, or Kelly Betting {see Glossary), you are maximizing your potential winnings while minimizing your risk.

Optimum Betting Strategy

How To Beat The Dealer At Any Casino

So, bottom line, how should you bet, based on your current advantage (or disadvantage)? The following table provides a list of true count optimal bets, which will work to your advantage in most multiple-deck games.

Looking at this table, you can find the maximum or optimum bet

True Count	Advantage	% Maximum
-1, or lower	-1.00%, or more	0%
0	-0.50%	0%
1	0%	0%
2	0.5% x 76%	.38%
3	1.0% x 76%	.76%
4	1.5% x 76%	1.14%
5	2.0% x 76%	1.52%
6	2.5% x 76%	1.90%
7	3.0% x 76%	2.28%

for any bankroll. All you do is multiply the figure in the last column by the amount of the bankroll. For example, for a bankroll of $5,000, the maximum bet you should make for a true count of 3 is .76 x $5,000 = $38.00.

The average gambler bets in units of $5, and that's what I recommend. Not only will you look like the average gambler, which will be to your advantage (more on that in Chapter 5), but $5 units are fairly easy to calculate. You also should understand that it is not possible to play only at shoes where the true count is constantly at +2 or higher, giving you the edge. Accept it now... you'll sometimes have to make a bet with a negative true count, when the house has the edge. In those circumstances, you can save a lot of money by leaving the table. However, never leave after winning a hand. Always leave the table after losing a hand. No casino will believe that a gambler would leave a table after a win.

Summary

Before you ever enter a casino, you need to, first of all practice, practice, practice counting cards, estimating the number of decks left to be played and calculating the true count. Besides mastering these proper playing techniques, you also need to establish a blackjack bankroll. Your bankroll should only be extra funds you set aside, solely for the purpose of gambling. If must be an amount that you can afford to lose without affecting your everyday lifestyle. In other words, don't gamble your rent money or your mortgage payment. If you have no extra money you can safely afford to risk, don't frequent a casino.

Money management as it relates to blackjack involves minimizing your loses while maximizing your gains. If you overbet to try and recoup a loss, you are playing right into the hands of the casino, and undermining prospects for long-term success. You

Chapter 5

Casino Secrets

will lose some of your bankroll. However, if you make your wagers based on the true count, in relation to when you have the advantage, your long-term success is all but guaranteed.

I f you've mastered the information presented in the preceding chapters, you already have an edge. In fact, you can already beat the dealer. But, from my own personal experience as a casino "eye in the sky" and as a player, I can assure you that beating the dealer and beating the casino are two entirely different matters. Sure, the dealer works for the casino, but he's not the one watching your every move from somewhere high above the table. That used to be my job — spotting the counters, and then turning them over to the floor supervisor and security.

If I saw that the counter was inept and entirely out of his league, I'd let him continue to play - unless by some miracle he started winning. My main instructions were to spot the professional counters — the ones who were actually good enough to cash in on their advantage. When I did, I would turn them over to my floor supervisor or the pit boss who told them to stay away from the blackjack table or ran them out of the casino altogether and told them to never come back.

In case you haven't caught on, let me say it straight out: Casino personnel, especially floor supervisors and pit bosses can not tolerate card counters playing at the blackjack tables. The reason is simple. The house knows that the game can be beaten by a skilled counter. And that scares them stiff. And it should. Imagine if everyone who played casino blackjack had mastered basic strategy and card counting. The house would seldom or never have the edge. So you can understand a casino's paranoia when it comes to card counting.

Depending on how severe the paranoia, a casino's reaction to a player who wins consistently and is suspected of being a dastardly card counter may vary from "keeping a close eye on the player" to kicking him out of, and barring him from the casino Even though our system is in no way cheating, the casino will treat you as if your are a cheater or an out and out crook. What that means is that a skillful player... a proficient counter must hide his abilities and appear as just another average gambler, all the while winning at the game.

While you may have mastered our system and have the ability to beat the dealer consistently, I'm sorry to tell you that's just the beginning. You'll have to learn the proper casino playing tactics to help you disguise your skills, and find additional methods and strategies to help improve your edge in the face of casino security. While your blackjack playing strategy may be perfect your gambling demeanor may get you booted right out of the casino.

In this chapter, I'll outline the techniques that I and many other successful players have used over the years to camouflage our skills as counters and help avoid being detected as winners by casino surveillance. I'll explain what to do and not to do in a variety of situations and scenarios, and above all, if you do get caught counting, exactly how to handle the situation to avoid get tossed out onto the street.

I've already explained how important it is that you practice and master the techniques of basic strategy and counting before you ever set down at a blackjack table. Well, friend, it is just as important that you learn some casino secrets that will enable you to come across, even under the most experienced scrutiny, as just another Joe. If a casino thinks you are a winner, then I can all but guarantee, you won't be for long.

Casino Counter Profiling

Beginning my very first day on the job as a "casino spy" several years ago, the floor supervisor drilled into me what to look for. From my perch in a little room in the ceiling above a major Las Vegas casino, I was paid ten-bucks-an-hour to spot card counters. I would spend hour after hour in front of a bank of video monitors watching the dealers deal...and the players play. Every day my supervisor impressed upon me her "profile" of the typical card counter. She believed counters could be spotted by their actions. Actually all casinos have prejudices against players they suspect of counting cards They are so paranoid that someone will get an advantage and actually beat the casino that they create a generally inaccurate, and unflattering profile of counters. Here's just a few of their prejudices, from their card counter's profile, I was given to work with:

■ Counters generally are young (mid-twenties to mid-thirties), white males (usually with beards).

■ Counters usually "check out" the tables in a pit, looking for a good count before joining a game.

■ A counter will change anywhere from $200 to $300 in chips and then bet only $5 or $10 on the fist hand.

■ Counters are unsociable. They don't talk to anyone. They just stare at the discard tray and rescan the table, checking the count.

■ A counter always places a minimum bet on the first hand of a newly -shuffled shoe.

■ A counter "thinks things over" before placing a bet.

■ Counters don't drink alcohol and they don't smoke.

■ A counter doesn't take insurance when he has a minimum bet out. However, he does take insurance when a big bet is out, regardless of his hand.

■ A counter never hesitates before playing a stiff hand.

■ Counters never tip the dealer.

Collectively, the above profile is a biased stereotype, born out of the casino's fear of losing money. Casinos don't like to lose money, and they'll go to great lengths to discourage it. That's why it's vital to your success as a counter to avoid what casino personnel consider suspicious behavior. There are a number of insider techniques you can use to do just that.

Card Counters' Camouflage

Obviously you can't make money at blackjack if you're not welcome at the casinos. If you fit the casino stereotype of a counter, you might as well hang a "Yes, I'm a counter and damn proud of it" sign around your neck. And then you might as well turn around and leave. It doesn't have to work that way. If you avoid a few beginners' mistakes, the casino personnel probably won't pay any extra attention to you at all. They'll think you are just another gambler out for a good time.

One thing to remember is that if you play for high states, you will be watched carefully, whether you win or lose. High-stakes players are always noticed, and given special "consideration" by the casino's "eye in the sky". But if you start with a recommended spread of $5 to $60, you probably won't come under very close scrutiny.

How often you play at a casino also can make a difference. You should try to spread your play around between casinos and shifts - Never play from one shift to another. And if you keep your sessions fairly short, the pit bosses won't be able to zero in on your action and figure out what you're doing (more on that later).

However, the real secret to camouflaging your true intent is to appear as though you are just another gambler. Here are some techniques I've used over the years with great success.

■ Dress like a gambler. I'm not talking about Kenny Rodgers here. But then again, that may not be too far off the mark. Casinos expect gamblers to frequent their tables. Indeed, they want gamblers for customers. A high-roller should look like a prosperous person, not some scruffy computer geek, or as a fellow counter once said "like an out of work substitute math teacher", playing for big money. Generally, counters dress like they are going to work (and of course, they are), in some cases wearing business suits, and others outfitted in casual wear, but not too casual for the money you're tossing around.

If you're going to a local casino on the day shift during the week, you should dress like a business person who is "getting away" from the office for a few hours. You want to look like someone who's just come in to gamble and have a good time... not like someone who doesn't really belong in a casino. That's a sure fire way to get the bosses' attention.

The key is to dress appropriately for

your betting level.

* Don't scout the tables in a pit, looking for a good count before joining a game. At least don't be conspicuous, if you do. Some players advocate the use of something called "back-counting" as a strategy for getting an advantage over the house before you even sit down at a table. Back-counting involves standing behind a game and counting down a pack. If the deck becomes favorable, you sit down and play. And I agree, that is a good way to begin play with an edge. However, it's also risky business. If the pit boss catches on to what you are doing, you'll likely be in for a quick exit.

One of the main problems associated with scouting the tables for a good count, or back-counting is purely logistical. Your view, when standing behind a game and trying to count down a deck, is generally obscured by the players. You have to be positioned just right to see all the cards. And you certainly can't stand behind a table all afternoon, waiting for a good count and chance to jump in the game. You'll begin to stick out like a sore thumb. And pit bosses become pit bulls when they suspect a counter on the premises.

That's why I recommend against scouting the tables, at least for beginners. When you enter a casino, just walk directly to a blackjack table where a dealer is shuffling the cards and sit down. Greet the dealer (and other players) in a friendly manner (at least say "hi").

■ Don't change a few hundred dollars into chips and then wager only $5 or $10 on the first hand. For example, if you're playing a game with a $5 minimum bet, buy in from $40 to $100. And when you are changing your $40 to $100 into chips, don't use terms like "nickels" or "quarters". Simply call the chips $5 or $25 chips.

■ Try not to spend a lot of time "thinking" about your bet. Remember the profile: only counters take time thinking about how much to bet. Real gamblers just shove their chips into the betting circle and wait for the dealer to give them a good hand. If you bust or got a natural, you should place your next bet as the dealer is playing his hand. With practice, and experience your next bet always will be the correct amount. It'll become automatic, and it won't appear as if you had to give it much thought.

The best way to disguise your betting strategy, and not give yourself away as a counter, is to always have a bet waiting in your betting circle.

n Be sociable. I realize that in the beginning, your focus will be on executing proper basic strategy and keeping count. However, you will call attention to yourself if you don't talk to anyone, and at least act as if you're having a good time just playing the game. Of course you need to look at the discard tray to count the number of decks played, but you shouldn't make it obvious that's what you're doing. Again, with experience, proper basic strategy and counting will become second nature. But in the beginning, you'll really have to work to disguise what you're up to.

■   Occasionally, you should take insurance against the dealer's ace when you have a minimum bet on the table. Don't ask for "even money". Just act like you aren't real sure how this "insurance thing" works. This act will serve to make the dealer slow down on his insurance calls later on, which will give you a little more time to calculate the true count. It's also a good idea to execute this "occasional" minimum insurance bet when a pit boss or floor supervisor is watching. It will reinforce their perception that you are simply a typical gambler and not a counter.

■   Hesitate, if only slightly, before hitting a stiff hand. Remember, professional counters never hesitate in such a situation. It's proper basic strategy. It's automatic. And that's just what will give you away. Playing like a counter. While you should automatically know to hit such a hand, pretend you are undecided - that you really aren't sure what to do. You may even be more convincing if you scratch your head and talk to the cards.

■ Tipping the dealer should be done sparingly. And when you do tip the dealer, wait until the count is high and you have a big bet on the table. Placing a bet for the dealer then will make it appear that you want him/her to help you win.

■ At least once in each session, begin a new shoe with a bet of 2 or 3 times the minimum.

■ Don't stray too far away from proper basic strategy in an attempt to disguise your play. You can use several "cover plays" (which I'll explain later) as a form of camouflage, but generally I recommend that you stick with basic strategy throughout your play. My experience has shown me that many casino personnel don't know that much about proper play, anyway.

■ NEVER leave a table after a win. That's not how gamblers play the game. If the count drops below -1, continue playing and making the minimum bet until you lose a hand. Then, excuse yourself and leave the table.

Cover Plays

How To Beat The Dealer At Any Casino

As I've already noted, some counters employ cover plays to throw casino personnel off the track when they're watching a little too closely. Most cover plays involve either bets or plays made at the wrong time — in relation to proper basic strategy and counting. For example, with a true count of +5, you'd like to make a big bet. However, if the floor supervisor has you in her sights, such a bet might be your last. It that situation, it might be as a former president used to say "prudent" to instead make a "cover bet" of a single unit. If your play is being scrutinized by the pit boss or other personnel, such a ploy is likely to throw them off the track if they too have been counting the game.

Another cover play you may use (again, sparingly) is to make a big bet right after the shuffle. Remember the profile again: "A counter typically will bet only the minimum on the first hand." That's because a counter knows (as do the casino personnel) that a player has no advantage off the top in a freshly shuffled session. Making a big bet in this situation is one way to, at least suggest to any pit personnel who may be watching you that you are not making your bet based on the count. In other words, by using this cover play you're telling the casino, to paraphrase another former president, "I am not a counter".

One more fairly popular cover play I've seen used by experienced counters involves deviating from proper basic strategy during the actual play of the hand. Again, this is a ploy I recommend that you use only sparingly, and then only when you have a small bet out. And it should be used only when you are certain that the casino is analyzing your play. As you should understand by now, deviating from proper basic strategy is not the way to win at blackjack. However, in some circumstances, deliberately making an incorrect play will take the heat off you and actually disguise your overall play. Keep in mind, however, that while incorrect play may throw the pit personnel off your track for a while, it will cost you money. So use this ploy wisely.

Generally, I recommend that you stick with proper strategy in all circumstances. Any deviation, whether it's in betting or actual play, will cost you money. Granted, it may help keep your true abilities and skills as a counter in disguise... for a while. But if you make such cover plays on a regular basis, you won't win in the long-run. So the result will be about the same as getting nailed as a counter. You lose.

The bottom line on cover plays. Use them sparingly, and then only when you are sure they will help your overall game.

What To Do If You Get Caught

No matter how good you play, how smooth or clever your act, you'll probably get nailed as a counter at least once or twice. It happens to the best players. During my days as "casino personnel" I saw many players get barred from the tables. And I can tell you that how a player responds to getting caught counting will determine whether or he/she will ever "play blackjack in this town again." That may sound somewhat melodramatic, but the truth is, that while getting barred from a blackjack table can be a traumatic experience, you've got to control your emotions, or you'll just make matters worse - a whole lot worse.

The best way to handle getting caught in the act, so to speak, is to avoid confrontation. Don't argue with the pit boss or anyone else. Just get up and leave as fact as you can. Remember, casinos don't like counters to begin with so you're not going to win any arguments. Don't try to convince the pit boss that you're innocent. You'll only be digging a deeper hole for yourself. You know you are a counter, and now you know the casino knows you are a counter. Protesting your innocence in such a situation can only result in further damage.

Just cash in your chips and make a speedy exit. And then, stay out of that casino for several months and off that particular shift for six months or more. When you do return, be cautious. If you sense any hint of recognition from the pit personnel, hit the bricks immediately. Don't press you luck. If the casino personnel do remember you from your last episode, you won't have a chance to win a dime. However, if you are patient, given time the casino will forget about you and move on to other suspected counters. Once that happens, you can sit back down at the table, and play your winning game again. Only, the next time DON'T GET CAUGHT!

How To Make Pit Bosses And Dealers Your Partners In Profits

To this point, you probably don't have a very favorable impression of casino personnel. You might think their primary goal in life is to keep you from winning. Well, that is a big part of their job, so you can't really fault them for being diligent and just doing what they are paid to do. However, pit bosses and dealers don't necessarily have to be your adversaries. In some circumstances, these people can actually be used to your advantage as a player.

First of all, let's consider the dealer. Most players, including counters engage in "toking" to varying degrees. Toking, which is casino language for tipping the dealer, is not a practice I recommend you use frequently or exorbitantly. It's a common mistake, especially when on a winning streak, not only to tip the dealer several times a session, but to overtip, as well. For instance, a player will win a $200 hand and then tip the dealer $25. That's a good size tip, and it generally doesn't buy you squat. Up front, tipping has an expectation of -100%. That is, if you tip the dealer, that money is gone. That's why many card counters never tip the dealer.

However, most dealers expect some tipping along the way, and it could actually be to your advantage to toke on occasion. For example, let's say as part of your act or camouflage, you want come across as a tourist or just a gambler who's in town looking for a good time. As part of your act, tipping the dealer may actually help to get the dealer on your side and allow you to play longer, under less scrutiny from the pit.

I'm not suggesting that by tipping the dealer you are actually paying for a guarantee of a winning session. That would appear to be collusion with the dealer, which is cheating and I have never, nor will I ever advocate cheating at any level. But I can tell you that most dealers (who, after all are only human) appreciate even modest tips. After all, it means extra money in his pocket.

Besides giving you some protection from the pit, toking also gives you an edge in other ways. For example, one of the best situations for toking is when a good count occurs near the end of the pack. If the dealer is undecided whether or not to shuffle, a timely toke on your part may persuade her to deal one more round. Obviously, with the count in your favor it's to your advantage to play that extra round.

How much and how often you should tip is a topic of some controversy. For my money (no pun intended), most players tend to overtip. And that's a good way to lose money, especially, if you toke several times an hour. A good rule of thumb I follow is to tip no more than 10% of your average bet, per hour. If you're betting $50 to $200, with an average bet of around $100, you'd be toking up to $10 and hour. While that's not an astounding hourly wage, most dealers accept it in the spirit in which it is given. At some level, they recognize that if you win, they win too, through your tips. And that's how, in some sense, you can make the dealer your partner in profits.

Getting a pit boss on your side, or at the very least to let you play without any heat, is a somewhat trickier situation. Obviously, a big part of a pit boss' job is to catch counters. That can make being "friendly" with them a somewhat awkward situation. However, pit bosses also are responsible for public relations and promotions involving the casino. And while some bosses are shall we say, overzealous in the "busting counters" part of their job, there are others who are more into the PR aspect. This type of pit boss is more interested keeping everybody happy and gambling. And that's the type of pit boss that you can use to your advantage.

The hard-nosed, "we don't tolerate no stinkin' counters in this casino" bosses, typically operate from a power base within the casino and are secure in their jobs. They'll toss you without blinking an eye. However, if you can find a boss who is perhaps new to the job or who is more interested in not making waves, you're in luck. This type of pit boss usually is more responsive and appreciative to friendly conversation (stroking, if you will) and compliments, because he doesn't feel completely secure in his job.

Whenever you find a pit boss that fits the latter description, you should make an attempt to cultivate a friendly, complimentary relationship. If you're successful, it could mean many hours of "heat-free" play.

How To Find The Right Casinos And The Right Games

Depending on what type of game you want to play and what house rules you favor, finding the right casino may require some legwork and some scouting around. One thing to consider is that conditions in most casinos can change on a daily basis. That's because the house is always experimenting, looking for a way to increase its edge. Unfortunately, blackjack seems to be a frequent victim of such experimentation. You might play at a table one day and it's all single deck. You go back the next day and find nothing but six-or eight-deck shoes. The point is, the house is always trying make it more and more difficult for players to win.

The result of this constant change is that you seldom know what type of game is being offered until you sit down at a table. The best way to find out what's going on and to find a casino with the type of game you want to play is to case the casinos before you play. By casing a casino, I mean casually strolling around the blackjack pits in a casino and watching what games are being played.

Since most of these big casinos are crowded with people, a casual casing shouldn't draw any unwanted attention from casino personnel. However, as I noted earlier, standing behind a table and counting down the deck, will most likely arouse suspicion. I've found it best to take a casual stroll around the pits, noting such things as how many decks are in play at each table, what the minimum bets are for each table, and which tables are getting the most scrutiny from the pit bosses.

Once I've mentally recorded the information I've gathered, I decide on which (if any) of the games I want to join. If there's nothing to my liking, I move on to the next casino and repeat the casing procedure. The point being that it's up to you the player to find the casino and game that's right for you. Don't just walk into the first casino on the strip and play any game being offered.

A Word About Cheating

You should understand by now that counting cards is not cheating, or against any law. However, since an expert counter can consistently beat the dealer, Casinos will do anything to stop counters - in some eases, even cheating. A few years ago while playing at a casino in a little tropical paradise I witnessed this casino tactic first-hand. I happened to notice that the dealer always kept his hand on the shoe, with his index finger on the next card to be dealt. At first I couldn't believe what I was seeing - he was dealing seconds, pulling back the top card to give himself a winning hand. Perhaps he was just a rogue dealer, or perhaps he was just following casino instructions. At any rate, I kept my mouth shut, lost a few hands and then made a quiet exit.

There actually are a number of ways a dealer can cheat, including stacked decks and marker cards, dealing seconds, and so on. However, I've only had the one personal experience so I'm never overly concerned about being cheated by the casino. I'm more concerned bout being nailed as a counter and barred from the casino. That's a much more likely scenario.

While being cheated by the casino is a possibility, you shouldn't assume that just because you're on a losing streak, the dealer is dealing dirty. Just keep your eyes open, your emotions under control, and your focus on strategy and counting, and you'll come out ahead in the long run.

Ten Things You Should Never Say At A Casino

Finally, even though you may be a skilled player and a master counter, you still must know how to know how to handle yourself properly in a variety of situations and scenarios. Here 's a lighthearted look at ten things you should never say at the card table.

1) "Could somebody tell me the count"?

2) "Mind if I sit out a few hands, and wait for the low cards to be played?"

3)"Excuse me, but could you leave the cards on the table a little longer after this hand?"

4) "Listen, I'm just learning this new card counting thing, so could you, maybe deal a little slower?"

5) "I'll trade you my 6 for your ace."

6) "Oops! Somebody get me a napkin and I'll clean my drink off the table."

7) "Ok dealer, let 'em fly. By my count, there are mostly tens and aces left."

8) "Let's see, where was I, oh yeah, plus two, plus one, zero, plus one ..."

9) "How much do you think I should bet?"

10) "Hang on a sec.... just let me take a gander at my strategy table."

Summary

Mastering basic strategy and the simplified counting system presented in this book will definitely give you a decided edge against any dealer at any blackjack table. However, the real secret to consistent winning at any casino is being able to disguise your playing skills. Otherwise, your playing time will be brief and unprofitable.

If you're serious about winning big money at blackjack, you must learn the proper casino playing tactics to help camouflage your abilities. Casinos are ever vigilant. They're always trying to identify and then eliminate counters, especially counters that beat them at their own game. If you learn and use the concepts and techniques described in this chapter, you can successfully disguise the skills you've learned throughout this book, and begin beating any casino at the blackjack table.

Blackjack Terms And Definitions

Action: The amount of money a player bets on all hands played. For example, if you play 50 hands of blackjack at $25 per hand, your action is $1,250.

Balanced System: A card-counting system in which the sum of the card values is equal to zero. Converting to a true count is required to make proper betting and playing decisions, with this system. The card-counting system described in this book is a balanced system.

Basic Strategy: The proper playing strategy based solely on the total of the player's hand and the dealer's upcard (See Chapter 2 Basic Strategy).

Blackjack/Twenty-One: A hand containing only an ace and a ten. Also called a natural.

Burn Card: After the cut, the dealer inserts the top card face up on the bottom of the deck or places in the discard pile. This is called burning a card, and the card used is called the burn card.

Bust/Break: To have a final card total greater than 21. When a player busts, he loses. When the dealer busts (card total exceeds 21) and the player does not, the player wins. If both the player and the dealer bust, the player loses.

Dealer: The casino, or house employee who deals the cards and conducts the game.

Discard Pile: The cards which are collected by the dealer after each hand are placed to the side in the discard pile.

Counter: A blackjack player who utilizes a system, which involves counting the cards in an attempt to gain an advantage in betting and making playing decisions (See Chapter 3 Card Counting).

Deck: Generally refers to 52 playing cards. A single deck consists of four aces, four each of 2 through 9 and sixteen 10s.

Double Down: A playing option which allows the player to double his bet and receive another card face down (See Chapter 1 Rules of Blackjack.).

First Base: The playing position immediately to the dealer's left. A player in this position receives cards before other players in the game.

Hard Hand: A hand without an ace, or any hand in which aces are counted as one. For example, 7, 8 is a hard 15; 6, 5, Ace is a hard 12.

Hit: To ask for another card from the dealer. The card received is called the hit card.

Hole Card: The dealers unexposed, or down card.

Insurance: A playing option that allows the player to make a side bet up to half his original bet. Insurance, or side bet is offered when the dealer's upcard is an ace. If the dealer has a natural, insurance pays the player 2:1.

Kelly Criterion: A method of betting wherein a player bets an amount in proportion to his advantage. Kelly betting requires that a player constantly re-evaluate his bankroll to order to properly calculate his next bet. The effect of betting based on Kelly Criterion is maximizing the players potential while minimizing the risk.

Late Surrender: A player must wait to surrender until after the dealer checks the hole card to see if his hand is a natural. If the dealer has blackjack, you many not surrender.

Natural: A two-card total of 21 — an ace and a 10-card — on the first two cards dealt. Also called blackjack.

Pack: Refers to the total number of cards in play. Generally, the term pack is used to refer to more than one deck of cards.

Pat: Any blackjack hand totaling 17 through 21. Such a hand does not require a hit.

Pit: The area of play in a casino, which generally is surrounded by blackjack and other gaming tables. Players typically wager from outside the pit while casino employees are stationed inside the bet.

Pit Boss: The casino employee in charge of the pit and subordinates (floormen, dealers, etc) working in the pit.

Press The Bet: Let winnings ride, along with the original bet.

Push: A tie between the player and the dealer. For example, both the player and the dealer have identical hands totaling 20. No money changes hands and the hand is called a draw.

Round: One round in blackjack includes making bets, dealing two cards to each player and the dealer, serving the players' hands, finishing the dealer's hand, and then making the payoffs.

Running Count: In card-counting systems this is the calculated result of each card based on the point value assigned to each card. This is an unadjusted count, which helps the counter determine the true count and in turn make proper betting and playing decisions.

Shoe: A box used by a dealer to hold cards that are being distributed to the players. The show usually is used in blackjack games that use more than two decks of cards.

Soft Hand: Any hand in blackjack in which the ace counts as 11. For example, Ace, 5 is soft 16.

Split: A blackjack playing option that allows the player to use each card of a pair as the first card of two separate hands (See Chapter 1 Rules of Blackjack.).

Stand: When a player chooses to play the cards he is dealt, not requesting a hit, he is said to stand.

Stiff: Any blackjack hand with a card total of 12 through 16.

Table Limit Or Maximum: The maximum amount which may be bet on one hand, excluding any extra bet on insurance, doubling down, or splitting.

Ten: Any card in blackjack that has a value of 10, specifically a 10, Jack, Queen or King.

Third Base: The seat at a blackjack table that is to dealer's immediate right. The player in this position is the last to receive cards from the dealer.

True Count: the running count adjusted to account for the proportion of the deck or shoe remaining to be played. Also known as the count per deck or point count index.

Twenty-One: Another name for blackjack.

You may cut this chart and keep it with you to review.

BLACKJACK BASIC STRATEGY MASTER CHART

PLAYER HAND	DEALER UP CARD									
	2	3	4	5	6	7	8	9	10	A
A & 2	H	H	H	D	D	H	H	H	H	H
A & 3	H	H	H	H	H	H	H	H	H	H
A & 4	H	H	H	H	H	H	H	H	H	H
A & 5	H	H	H	H	H	H	H	H	H	H
A & 6	H	D	D	D	D	H	H	H	H	H
A & 7	D	D	D	D	D	D	D	D	D	H
A & 8	D	D	D	D	D	D	D	D	D	D
A & 9	H	H	S	S	S	H	H	H	H	H

H = Hit   S = Stand   Sp = Split   D = Double

PAIRS

PLAYER HAND	DEALER UP CARD									
	2	3	4	5	6	7	8	9	10	A
22	SP	SP	SP	SP	SP	SP	H	H	H	H
33	SP	SP	SP	SP	SP	SP	H	H	H	H
44	H	H	H	SP	SP	H	H	H	H	H
55	D	D	D	D	D	D	D	D	H	H
66	SP	SP	SP	SP	SP	H	H	H	H	H
77	SP	SP	SP	SP	SP	H	H	H	H	H
88	SP	SP	SP	SP	SP	SP	SP	SP	SP	SP
99	SP	SP	SP	SP	SP	SP	S	SP	SP	SP
10S	S	S	S	S	S	S	S	S	S	S
AA	SP	SP	SP	SP	SP	SP	SP	SP	SP	SP

Upcard: The dealer's exposed, or face-up card.

<u>Hard Hand Basic Strategy</u>
You may cut this chart and keep it with you to review.

Figure 1   **S = Stand**   **H = Hit**

Player Hand	Dealer's Up Card									
	2	3	4	5	6	7	8	9	10	Ace
17	S	S	S	S	S	S	S	S	S	S
16	S	S	S	S	S	H	H	H	H	H
15	S	S	S	S	S	H	H	H	H	H
14	S	S	S	S	S	H	H	H	H	H
13	S	S	S	S	S	H	H	H	H	H
12	H	H	S	S	H	H	H	H	H	H
4-11	H	H	H	H	H	H	H	H	H	H

<u>Soft Hand Basic Strategy</u>
You may cut this chart and keep it with you to review.

FIGURE 2

Player Hand	Dealer's Up Card									
	2	3	4	5	6	7	8	9	10	Ace
A,8-10	S	S	S	S	S	S	S	S	S	S
A,7	S	S	S	S	S	S	S	H	H	H
A,2-6	H	H	H	H	H	H	H	H	H	H

S= Stand   **H= Hit**

How To Beat The Dealer At Any Casino

Hard Hand Double Down Stretegy
You may cut this chart and keep it with you to review.

Figure 3   **Double Down A Hard Hand**

Player Hand	Dealer's Up Card									
	2	3	4	5	6	7	8	9	10	Ace
12	D	D	D	D	D	D	D	D	D	D
11	DD	DD	DD	DD	DD	DD	DD	DD	DD	D
10	DD	DD	DD	DD	DD	DD	DD	DD	D	D
9	DD	DD	DD	DD	DD	D	D	D	D	D
8	D	D	D	D	D	D	D	D	D	D

DD = Double Down   **D = Don't Double Down**

Figure 4   **Double Down A Soft Hand**

DD = Double Down   **D = Don't Double DownDD**

Player Hand	Dealer's Up Card									
	2	3	4	5	6	7	8	9	10	Ace
A ,8,9	DD	DD	DD	DD	DD	DD	DD	DD	DD	DD
A,6-7	DD	D	D	D	D	DD	DD	DD	DD	DD
A, 4-5	DD	DD	D	D	D	DD	DD	DD	D	D
A, 2-3	DD	DD	DD	D	D	DD	D	D	D	D

= Double Down   **D = Don't Double Down**